Tina Daniels is thirteen years old and she is a star. She can sing and dance. Everyone knows her. Everyone loves her. They call her 'Curls' because she has beautiful curly hair. They all want her photo. She can have anything she wants.

But is she happy?

Does she want to be a star?

"Tina, why are you eating chocolates?" her mother asks. "I like them. They're nice!" Tina says. "You're getting fat, and a fat girl doesn't get lots of money in Hollywood," Mrs Daniels says. "You want the money – I don't!" Tina says.

Tina is angry with her mother and Mrs Daniels is angry with Tina. Tina leaves the room and cries.

Tina is very sad. She does not want to be a star. She
wants a quiet life. One day she has an idea. Her
schoolfriend, Mary, has a grandmother called Mrs
White. Old Mrs White lives in the country, in
Stonechurch. Tina has a photo of Mary in front of Mrs
White's house. It looks very pretty – not like the city!
Tina decides to go there.

Tina is at the city station. She is wearing jeans and an old jumper. People do not know who she is.

"Where do you want to go, young girl?" the man at the ticket office asks her. "Stonechurch, please. When's the next train?" Tina asks. "The train leaves at two o'clock from platform three," the man says. Tina buys her ticket.

Tina arrives at Stonechurch. She sees an old house near the river. It is the house in the photo! There are flowers and trees in the garden.

"Mrs White must live here," Tina thinks. She goes to the front door and rings the bell. An old lady with white hair and a kind face opens the door. A black cat comes out too.

"Good afternoon, who are you?" the old lady asks.
"Oh, hello, Mrs White. My name is Tina. I'm a
schoolfriend of your granddaughter, Mary." "Mary's
schoolfriend – how nice to meet you! What are you
doing in Stonechurch, Tina?" Mrs White asks. Tina says
she hates the city life. "Well," says Mrs White, "come in
and have a cup of tea, my dear."

6

Tina and Mrs White drink tea and talk. Mrs White does
not know Tina is a star. She does not have a television or
a radio. Tina is very happy! Mrs White says, "Tina, you
can stay with me for a week, but first you must
telephone your mother." Tina is angry with her mother
and doesn't telephone her. "Mother says yes!" she says
to Mrs White later. Her face is a little red.

Two days later Mrs White is taking Tina for a walk.

"Look at the lambs!" Mrs White says.

"Yes, I love them. I want to be a lamb. They can jump and run and be happy."

"You can run and jump and be happy too, Tina."

"No, I can't. I –"

"Tina, you're young. Run!"

Tina is living a very different life in the country. She sees new things all the time.

Now it is night, and Tina and Mrs White are waiting. It is very quiet. Every night some hedgehogs come to the garden. Mrs White puts out food for them.

"I love their long brown noses," Mrs White says. "So do I," says Tina.

"Oh, look!" says Tina.

A big brown fox is running across the garden. At first
Tina is very happy to see the fox. There aren't any foxes
in gardens in the city! Then she sees the fox has
something in its mouth. The 'something' is Mrs White's
chicken! Mrs White is very angry and wants to kill the
fox!

Mrs White and Tina look at the fox's work. The
chickens are making a terrible noise. "We can't have
eggs for breakfast in the morning, Tina," says Mrs
White. "Why not?" asks Tina. "The chickens aren't
very happy. When they aren't happy they can't give us
eggs," Mrs White explains.
For breakfast Tina has toast and fresh orange juice.

Three days later Tina is with Bella, the horse. She loves
Bella and gives her some sugar.

Today the postman has a letter for Mrs White. When he
sees Tina, he says, "I don't believe it – it's Curls!" Then
he says to her, "Everyone's looking for you. You're in all
the newspapers!" He runs to his red van to find his
newspaper.

Mrs White reads the postman's newspaper.

"Tina," says Mrs White, "you're the *'LOST TV STAR'*,
aren't you! I don't understand . . . Your mother . . ."

"Yes, I'm Curls, but please don't send me home. I'm
happy here with you."

"I'm coming with you to see your mother. I've got a
good idea," Mrs White says.

Tina's mother is very happy to see Tina again. Mrs White explains her idea: Tina can go to her friend's school on the island of Guernsey, between England and France. Tina can have friends there who do not know she is Curls.

"What? I want Tina to be a star!" Mrs Daniels says.

"She wants to be happy," Mrs White says quietly.

Tina is at school in Guernsey. She has new friends and new interests. One day, Tina's friend is reading a magazine. It is about film and television stars. There are lots of beautiful photos of beautiful people. Everyone looks very happy. "What a wonderful life!" the friend says. Tina smiles to herself. "Who wants to be a star?" she says. "I don't."

### Questions

1 Why do people call Tina 'Curls'? (*page 1*)

2 Why is Tina angry with her mother? (*page 2*)

3 What is Tina wearing? (*page 4*)

4 How long can Tina stay with Mrs. White? (*page 7*)

5 What does Tina see in the garden? (*page 9*)

6 Why is Mrs White angry? (*page 10*)

7 Who finds out Tina is a star? (*page 12*)

8 What island does Tina go to? (*page 14*)

### Puzzle

Unmix the letters to find the right word.

I E U B U A T F L

S A R K B F E A T

G Y A R N

G E E H O S D G H

P E P N S W A E R

### Ideas

1 You are a star for one day. Write about what you do, where you go, who you meet.

2 Choose a film or pop star you want to be. Ask a friend to interview you about your likes and dislikes. They can use a cassette recorder.

3 Draw or paint a picture of Mrs White's garden.